The
Unexplored Ocean

T0158475

To my father,
already voyaging.

The
Unexplored Ocean
Catherine Fisher

seren

seren
is the book imprint of
Poetry Wales Press Ltd.
First Floor, 2 Wyndham Street
Bridgend, Mid Glamorgan
Wales, CF31 1EF

© Catherine Fisher, 1994

British Library Cataloguing In Publication Data:

Fisher, Catherine
The Unexplored Ocean
I. Title
821.914

ISBN: 1-85411-106-X

The publisher acknowledges the financial assistance of the Arts Council of Wales.

Cover: Watercolour of *The Resolution* by Henry Roberts, courtesy of The Mitchell Library, Sydney, Australia.

Printed in Palatino by Redwood Books, Trowbridge

Contents

Monument To Captain Hardy, Blackdown Hill.

Your memorial is shorter, and more rustic;
it lacks the tapering elegance, the lions,
but there's no doubt it has the better view.

Ironic, for you towered over him,
helped him on with his coat, cut the meat on his plate;
were the only one who bothered to visit his wife.

He would have envied you the sea,
the long sweep of Chesil, the hiss and clatter
of stones dredged by the water and the moon.

And Portland, that thrust fist of land;
remember how it dwindled as you sailed,
and both of you watched, in the bluster and flap of the canvas.

He knew, that last time. That voyage
his preparations were more thorough than before;
the will, the letters, the prayer in the locked book.

"Perhaps a leg this time" he said, with that
twisted smile. And the men around the table silenced,
the wine in their glasses listing slowly to starboard.

Unsentimental, you measured him,
his vanity, his foolish delight in titles,
that ruthlessness with ships, — but not with men,

saw how he bound them to him with a word,
a soft enquiry, a grave nod of the head —
the rough old salts who joked with him as he passed.

The news took sixteen days to get to England.
Bells were rung, audiences stood in theatres
to applaud his laurelled portrait descending on wires.

And you were leaning cold and cloaked on the taff-rail;
under you Victory red and soiled and broken;
around on the sea, wreckage, and his prayer in your pocket.

Black Dog

It waits by motorways, and the verges of lanes.
Drivers have seen it on wet winter nights,
sudden, in the flash of headlights.
Look back and it's gone.

Late stragglers by the church report it
padding the grey road.
It passes by and does not turn its head;
paws deep in the crisp, wet leaves.

They say it's growing, our hound, our sinister
companion. Someone
must have loosed that chain
of reason and laughter.

Its eyes are crystal and molecule. Already
it's bitten a chunk out of the sky.
It licks trees and they wither.
The black slick of its paw stirs and sullies the seas.

When it has grown enough watch it then,
swell to bursting, roar, devour the sun,
in the silence nose the small bones on the sand,
the dead moon glinting in its eyes.

Marginalia

The wind pushes snow through the gap under the door;
ices each stalk of grass and marram.
On days like this the birds drop,
the vole flattens itself on the tunnel floor.

Fintan has taken to putting out crumbs,
stale bannocks — the grey geese scream for them.
Father Abbot wonders if such creatures have souls.
They both know the granary is empty.

Yesterday I dropped the golden cup,
my fingers were too numb.
Wine flooded the cracks on the floor.
Reverent, we lifted a cobweb of blood.

And sometimes at dusk when the candle flickers
the tapestries move.
Dogs and stag ripple and run
down the green hills of the fraying cloth.

The hound and the stag in the margins of my book
on paths of knotwork, under and over,
chase their joyful, unending chase.
Carefully, I draw their gold threads.

They say Columba spoke with angels;
was once a prince in a warm house.
When he died his hands were blistered,
swollen with the ague and the world's rain.

The tide falls; at the fen's edge
it coats the stubble with ice like glass;
a new layer at each ebb, bubbled and gritty;
inside, the green blade, feeling no wind.

Archaeology: Four Seasons

I. Winter

Six days before Christmas
and the ground is iron.
If the lids of the ditches are smashed
they reform with thin
linkages of water.

We crowd the caravans
washing pot,
burning broken brushes in the fire.
I wear gloves within gloves,
fingers in fingers.

Sometimes the wild girl, Annette,
heats the poker,
plunges it into the brown
muddy water. It hisses
like a dragon

but the heat fades quickly,
into air,
into numbness.
On a curled calendar
the days are slashed with blue.

Speech is if, and when.
Speech is tomorrow.
Speech is what we will do,
is red, heated,
steaming and spicy,

sharp as holly, bright
as tinsel;
while the brushes lick
corners and edges,
smooth curves, fragments of feasts.

II. Spring

And leaning on the mattock Michael said
"Imagine the silence there must have been"
and we stood, easing cramped knees
and the pain in the back,
hearing behind the hum of cars
the stillness of a valley deep in woods,
not measured yet, not sounded,
the long curled snake of its river
asleep in the red mud,
the world a green untrodden tangle
from here to Rome.

Then a plane roared over Wentwood
unzipping the blue hours,
and we shovelled the past into barrows,
the air trembling on our shoulders.

III. Summer

He's remembering his time in Equador,
the flashing birds in the forest,
the flowers, red wells of scent and honey.
We nod, and are silent.
We've heard it before.

In ten months we have dug out all obsessions,
have talked ourselves out into grunts,
the silent endurance of the weather,
the quip, the nickname,
the slow grin of mockery.

Above him a cormorant hangs its wings to dry.
The sun's hand is heavy on my back.
A slice of the soil shows
Samian, smashed like
egg-shell in the ditch.

He stands up, and flexes his shoulders,
says he's known heat that kills.
On the smooth orange bowl is a dancer.
She looks up at him,
as if she listens.

IV. Autumn

When the girl wrote in her notebook
rain magnified the words,
smeared them, made ignorant
blue-tinted tears of them.

"And when you dig" she said "what
do you expect to find?"
and she looked at the field with
its lid off, the moonheaps of spoil.

The barrel, but not Diogenes.
The sword, but not Arthur.
The darkness gives back no thoughts or speech.
Grief and legend are no part of her.

"When we dig we find ourselves
whatever we look for."
The answer came from the back,
the girl wrote it down,

and it was a good answer too,
though not to her question.
We looked at each other and smiled.
Next season we may start another field.

Frozen Tarn

Some queen has left her mirror on the grass.
If I could pick it up the back
would be metal, the chased whorl and counter-whorl,
all the mystic twisting.

She's left it tilted, reflecting
the dark fringe of trees
and the grey huddle of hills.
Her mirror holds the only empty spaces.

One of those women from the ancient tales
— the tragic, defiant ones —
always with a witty answer on their tongues
and usually some secret in a tower room.

A cold oval of myth on the winter hillside,
and you, far down there
bending over, stepping out on her polished treachery,
balanced on a moving iron cloud.

Field-walking

Field-walking. A line
strung across the redundant furrows,
advancing foot by foot
through wet rags of turnip,
clods of red, unbreakable
Monmouthsire clay.
We are beaters in a grim hunt,
our quarry a white oyster shell,
a nail, a splinter of pot.
The wind, our hound,
is leaping between us,
snatching away our sparse remarks,
worrying them into the ditch.
We are stiff with stooping,
giddy with gleaning; behind us
the valley spins in its coat of rain.
And when one stops, kneels,
the line pauses, tugged to
stillness by our rope of instinct,
each head turning in the wind,
the collars of our coats rising like hackles.

On the Third Day

And the Carpenter said "I shall make a machine
that will filter the air clean of its poison;
that will pump and drag up water
from the deep rocks to the sky; a guardian of rainbows,
that will hold the soil steady, knotting it tight
with invisible, intricate webbing.
A machine that will surfeit a million insects,
hold the birds and the climbing tribes of apes;
a protection for my sons against wind and lightning,
a fuel that will heat their hands and faces;
whose by-products will be ships, and violins, and gallows;
whose shavings will be stained with my children's names,
their truths slowly discovered, their gorgeous lies,
their fingers' deftness with blue and gold and ochre.
My machine will cause poets to make verse,
will smell like honey and rain and ashes;
will break out yearly in a rash of apples;
will unleash a million berries.
I will call it oak, and beech and thorn;
I will design it in a thousand shapes and places,
and I will give it to my sons for their salvation
— let them guard it well.
On the day the sun dies and the rain is bitter
I will come and hang my sorrows from its branches.

Tapestry Room

The edge of the moon is unravelling.
Run your finger down the clouds and brambles,
the soft, fraying silken owls.
Stags leap russet from a fungal forest
drained to a grey that drifts at the touch,
hanging on the spears of light thrust through it.

We breathe this in, it clogs our syllables,
tastes on our tongues; a skilled
fingerwork dissolving in our draughts.
Feel it on your skin, its faint
fur on your lips; see on the floor
how you've printed your pathway across it.

They all wove it, wove themselves into it,
a web of the tales and tellers
so we might loosen the woven hours like spore;
drifting out of themselves into rooms,
into echoes, into those who listen,
into a dust of moon and feathers in your voice and eyes.

Spells

There are the concoctions made from herbs;
marigold, feverfew and honey, anointing
forehead and eyes. There are words
said softly in fields, circling against the sun.
Not forgetting blue petals, apple-peel over the shoulder,
wand and pentangle's false promises;
brown smoke in a mirror,
obscuring the twisted figure in the glass.
Think too, of sudden silences in theatres,
any mutual knowledge, shared vision;
the dance of sword blades; the faint blur
and drone of wasps on a hot afternoon.
And then above all these the mind's glass tower,
where the wizard sleeps among his treasures.

Merlin on Ynys Enlli

It would have taken more than Nimuë
— the poets' sweet ensnaring jade —
to spin the net that could entangle me.
I sailed here in a grey December,
my cloak patched, salt in my beard.
No star lit my track across the water.

I built my palisade of glass
among the boulders and coarse sand,
the kelp and marram grass.
The wind brought ice
and shells and moonlight to my hands.
The earth gave bone; the gulls their cold cries.

My tower is tall; it will have many windows.
Three doors open on each side
where I will stand and watch the slow
waves thunder in the crannies of the cliff.
My house is not shaken by the tide.
It casts no shadow; the stranger will not see it.

Here I will hoard my thirteen shining treasures,
against the mountains dwindling, grain by grain,
against the darknesses between the stars.
And only the drowning fisherman in the storm,
torn in the appetite of squall and rain,
will see that wand of light come sliding from my door.

Incident at Conwy

(During the Wars of the Roses a Lancastrian officer was shot by a marksman stationed on the battlements of Conwy Castle. The river between them was at least half a mile wide. The feat was recorded by several chroniclers.)

1. Llewelyn of Nannau

Oh man you are foolish to wear that surcoat.
The gold and the blue outrage the dull afternoon.
You are a heraldic flicker among the leaves
tempting my pride.
I have not killed men in the stench and fury
of battle only, that I would baulk at this.
I am an archer. I send death winging,
sudden and cold over parapet and fosse;
the lightning that strikes nowhere twice.
I'm too far away to see your pain,
the blood that will sully that bright coat;
too far for the shriek from your lady's arbour.
Nor will imagination spoil my aim.
The taut string creaks against my fingers,
brushes my cheek softly, as I draw back.
My eye is steady down the shaven shaft.
You're a roebuck, a proud stag, a target.
Your words do not goad me, I can't hear what you say.
Your death will be skilfully given, and without rancour.
At least I am not too far from you for that.

2. Rhys ap Gruffudd Goch

The river is wide, and the leaves cover us.
We are safe enough, but they are certainly ready
— each tower and arrowslit is crowded with faces,
and notice the fool on the battlements with his bow.
This castle will drink an oblation of blood
before we break its stone teeth.

That archer has seen me; he lifts his bow.
Well the river will not bleed from his arrow.
Doubtless he would kill me if he could
and boast about it over the spilled wine;
a distant, stout, nameless man
who would never have seen my face.

Then he would thresh about in the straw at night
seek solace from priests, drink away memory,
but the line would have been thrown between us,
the bright gift passed, that he could not take back.
Look, he draws. If he should strike me down
I will never be so far from him again.

Winterfyllith

(The Saxon month of October)

The spiders first of all, the spiders
come clogging the corners of autumn,
jerking down from flooded gutters;
safety nets strung with
small glass light-bulbs after rain.

They are followed by the leaves,
that silent unfastening. Soil is damp,
the long wet grass will not dry out,
nor the brown stems of herbs, the fungi's
spiral staircase round the rotting tree.

Fat woodcock thump down in the furrows,
back from their summer on the moon.
Hard blue sloes are snapped,
crushed in baskets for gin or jelly.
The darker nights of forecasting begin.

Sliced apple-peel, herbal candles
smoking in mirrors, all the omens
gather to their close. The month's end
is a bonfire and a bolted door,
and a new blackness breathing round the house.

Burne-Jones' Angels

He lets the pen unwind its line of figures,
drifting down the stairways of the air;
outlines the shawm and psaltery, the lilies.
Sometimes he thinks that angels are like this,
faces of grave beauty without passion,
that do not speak, are never less than perfect,
that have no white-hot hunger for his soul.
But on the lonely evenings when the moon
lays a light finger on his empty hands,
he wonders if he might not have betrayed them,
made of love a decorative device,
an easy image of the unbearable.
And looking through the window at the trees
he knows he never could do otherwise,
that his art tells all its truth with lies.

Llanddewi Fach

Today to the green hill
comes a wind from the isle of apples;
from Rome and Iona
and the Skirrid's red soil;
an ice wind that brings rain and spiders
and the uneasy hum of cars from the valley road.

Down there the web of names
is pegged on the hillsides; Cadoc and Cybi,
Tegfedd, Teilo, slender Cenedlon;
those relentless walkers in the rain,
spinners of words and the net of breath,
scatterers of stones and crosses in the land's crannies.

Who speaks their language?
Who would understand them
here where the tide of that tongue has ebbed,
left their foundations
stark as the ribs of a stranded ship,
their names studding the woven speech of strangers.

They left us a bedrock
of bones and memories,
the ploughed field and the word,
the blunt word we have not spoken.
If they were here what would they say to us?
With what scraping of syllables could we answer them?

***

Behind the church some white hives blister.
Bees hum in their broken slats
speared by grass and gargoyle shadows.

Toppled, overgrown,
towers of Babel fallen silent,
softening into the moist soil.

Let's say this is another dereliction;
the loss of a different harvest.
Honey that will never be gathered

oozing through the hands,
its sweetness dropping into jars;
the stung fingers, the soft, vivid aroma.

Listen. There is thunder in the valley.
Among the leaves come the patterings
of rain, each leaf

heavy with its wart of water.
In the green cascade,
the dance of sepal and stalk,

a mile of hedgerows drips to Llandegfedd
and, silent as chance, the Sor
sips swollen mosses.

Each flower in the county
is weighted with its raindrop,
fat and heavy as a glass bee.

**

Rain on the tiles and the leaning wooden slats,
battering doors to a green dust,
splitting the timbers with its cold wedges,
raising on the path green spears to ring in this castle.

Theirs has been a long siege.
They have grown too much alike,
as enemies do who face out over the walls
learning, year by year, each others moods and movements.

Dust and spore, the floating mycelium
is knitting them back,
webbing them tight, the llan and the planet
as they were, before the spade went in, before the schism.

***

Now Maelduin on his voyage would have forced the door,
and as it crumpled into clouds
would have waited in the dust and sunlight,
all his men clustered at his back,
letting silence settle like a spell;
as if a sorcerer hid somewhere on the hillside
and had not left his house without its guard.

Or Odysseus would have slid inside,
his salt-stiff jerkin scraping the white wall,
eyes on the cobwebs and the toppled chair,
his mind back in the palace he had seen
stripped of its gold and tapestries;
the wine-cup rolling on the floor,
the fallen king led down the empty street.

Most travellers touch this place;
an island of silence and green shade,
a place to linger, and leave slowly.
This is no-one's destination,
but long after they think they have come home,
lying awake in the early morning

or leaning on the quayside in the rain,
this will be the moment they remember,
as if they almost arrived at something here,
but the tide turned, or the wind banged a door,
or the sound of a footstep hurried them away.

***

Down there, look, the cars are journeying
through tunnels of blackberries;
past girls in green and the scarlet rowan,
hips and haws and sting
of nettles; leaving spiders
in the slipstream swinging in their nets;
through the hedgerow's rich imagery of affliction,
its berry-blood and thorns.

Now all the roads lead elsewhere,
and only a few come back.

In their wake the air is awhirl with seed;
white fluff and pips, drifts
of spore, winged keys twisting
from the unlocked trees;
and all this cascade
and flaunt and spin scattered
on soil and on stony ground
and into the sunroofs and the lifting hair of girls.

We have flung the future in handfuls
from these lost hills.

Centuries after we have stood here
the grey lift of the roof will mark our design;
winter will bring frost

and the spring's green fingers prize
us open, crack us wide
and grow up through
and our words will be carried away
like the seed in the cars down the lanes

but they will not return to us empty,
or in any translation.

Pencils

Six, in a box of Chinese lacquer,
smelling of sandalwood,
each in its roll of marbled paper.

One for a neglected letter;
whims, an arbitrary mood
stroked to that deft, unchanging order.

One for sketching the blown boughs,
quickly, in haste,
fixing the season's throes.

And the poem will claim one, that's sure;
selfish, it will waste
itself, eat itself up with pleasure.

The fourth on a plan of fields will mark
secret places; a gate
in a lane for leaning on, a tree by a lake.

Another will weave a story; reason
and folly in a tight net.
This too will entrap the seasons.

The last is a silent danger.
Let it lie like a wand.
One day I'll open the box and unleash its power.

Poem for David Lewis

(d. 27 August 1679)

...I believe you are met here to hear a fellow-countryman speak...

You spoke Welsh on the scaffold;
the Usk men understood you.
They would not now.
The local executioner locked his door;
it was a stranger who tightened your
tourniquet of rope,

and then they held him back till you were dead;
would not let the worst be done.
They created saints in their own image;
small men, cunning and discreet,
saints of the kitchen and the gentry's table,
compassionate, unassuming.

David Lewis, priest, Welshman,
wearer of disguises,
look at your grey town and swollen river,
the churches and the muddy lanes,
the houses whose dark hiding-holes you knew.
Look at your people, David,

the women and the young men who still kneel
and kiss the cold unchiselled granite
that marks your March, your borderland,
the bruising ground of language gainst language,
where the rough rope necklace dropped,
and strangled speech.

Gwern-y-cleppa

There's a squall prowling up the estuary,
piling clouds on the moon.
The wood is a black promise,
an emptiness.
Here's a place where everything's uneasy.

In its tangle of branches I'm a shadow
fumbling foot by foot
down aisles of alder;
a stumbler
in a room of roots and hollows.

I hold the moment with both hands,
but it's gone in the
rustle of leaves, the roar
of the cars
in the cleft below Graig-y-Saeson.

Now you, Dafydd, would have known
how to keep it, how to hammer
an armour from such nothings, the bright
hard words
intricately linked; the chain

that stops no sword. I wonder
how you'd recognize it,
all your green Wales, its welcome
of a poem
with a coin and some honour.

Darkness itself is not the same;
the hill sliced deep
to its red heart. And the moon
brings rain,
and even that has the touch of the betrayed.

Still I've come, to the hall of stems,
to ask whatever you can give.
Image of earth and leaves, a rhythm,
a word or two, I'll take them,
carry them home, hidden,

with a rueful kind of pride;
my gifts from a generous patron;
as the moon floods lost windows
with its silver,
lighting the way through the wood.

Words

They are stones
shaped to the hand.
Fling them accurately.

They are horses.
Bridle them;
they'll run away with you.

They are windows,
opening on vistas
that are unreachable.

They are apples.
Bite on hardness
to the sweet core.

They are coracles;
flimsy,
soon overloaded.

They are candles.
Carry them carefully.
They have burned cities.

Untitled

Promises and oaths; stories and evasions;
all the apparatus of the pen;
setting traps for myself, giving myself conditions;
the silence you left has made me glib again.

Now, like Conaire Mor in the old story
I see the three red riders of my fate,
leading me over the moor to the iron bothy,
where all the words I've written lie in wait.

Those Who Make Paths

Here's a song of praise for all those people
who live at the forgotten edge of things;
who come out at night and take long walks
under the lamp-posts, remembering;
women who stay behind to clean old churches,
rubbing the shining faces week by week,
speaking their thoughts to angels and the dead,
a silent congregation at their back.

Men who go out in the early morning
to gather sticks from urban river banks;
old men with allotments, or with bikes
piled with panniers of spuds;
women who push home-made carts or carry
wood on prams, grandchildren riding high
and sucking kaylee. Where are they
in the world's eye?

And those who make the paths that run through hedges,
through the corners of fields, who leave charred
sticks and charcoal deep in hidden copses;
kids who dream in corners of the yard;
anglers, and cyclists going nowhere really
but away, happy to be alone;
those who live beneath the world's dignity;
those who've been poets, and have never known.

Teyrnon Looks at Gwent Iscoed

High on this hill I feel the warm earth
murmur, see the drivers down there
slice through the winding ways,
through stories
they won't let the land re-tell.

All my kingdom's marked with spoor
and spraint and paw-print;
the legends I have hunted over her;
beast and saint,
forgotten battles lost under the hedges.

Boundary between voices, ways of speaking,
tethered to England by a silver chain
a second in the forging;
a place
to pass through, wary for the snares.

A people not like any other people;
scornful of Welsh and Sais,
ignoring at dusk in the lanes the prints
of impossible beasts,
but taking the old way home, in case.

No Other Language

There is no other language but the sea's,
speaking the world's first words and memories;
chuckling and splashing deep within its throat
the truths it told before the fishes came,
when secret and alone it smoothed the sand
and wrote and rubbed the lost words out
that no-one understands.

There is no other question but the sea's,
asked always of the sailor and beachcomber,
in the current of the moving blood,
the opening and closing of the moon,
the fluid dreams, the heart's rhythm and flow;
and those who hear it have no words
to answer now.

There is no other breathing but the sea's,
lying awake all night under the stars,
rising and falling, the smooth rocks
under a fringe of weed, the skeletons
of broken spiral shells rubbed smooth as bone;
its dreams of shoals and currents and drowned wrecks
deep as our own.

Elegy 1

You made them that last summer, prints
of bare feet in the hard wet sand,
good prints, prints that anyone might follow.
And on the rippled patches between rocks
where the sea lays down its silent patterns
the ridges were hard under your heels.
How many tides have emptied since
on the cleansed, uneasy, drifting land,
endlessly destroying and re-making
grains and shoals and silts,
sifting strata to a slow, wet sludge?
Collision of two powers since life's beginning
— land's endurance, sea's wild energies —
grinding all our prints away between them,
making a place where neither can quite rule;
a borderland, a narrow bank where nothing roots
and even tiny things that live hang on,
tossed from breath to breath and wave to wave,
gripping with muscled ligaments of flesh
against the drag of soft, dissolving sands.

Elegy 2

Since the new window, the front door looks strange.
The old glass had been in there since we came;
bubbled, so that no-one could see out.
Then late one night a street kid threw a stone.
You always meant to change it, but the black
spiderweb of cracks hung there for weeks
through the freezing winter of your sickness.
They carried you past it to the waiting car.

The new glass is lighter, has another pattern,
makes the street look less contorted,
lets us see the postman bring the letters.
A glazier came to fit it; he was messy,
not like you would have been. If you knocked
now, we'd look different as we answered.

Flood

Now the rain falls on her outspread fingers.
High in the window she lets the droplets spill
into nettles and poppies,
rolling from leaf to earth.
If the flood came now, relief.

If it came trickling and rippling up the walls,
drowning the gate, the holes in the path,
roses in their barricade of thorns;
the flood that covers all identities
would bring her peace.

All her harps would hang upon the willows,
songs snagged on brambles, slowly drowned,
and high up in the attic of her house
she'd leave the photograph, the broken toy
for the water to destroy.

Over the fields the flood with silver fingers
would pick the locks and open all the windows,
rummage in the spaces of the heart;
steal the heap of days and drown them deep
and she'd sleep, she'd sleep.

Custodian

Somehow they opened an abyss inside me.
All day, if I looked up, their eyes
mocked me down the gallery, slyly

behind strangers, over people's shoulders.
If I tried to read they'd slow my thoughts to silence.
Later, on the rainy afternoons above the downpour

I'd hear them at the far end of the room,
murmuring, their words too indistinct.
Often I heard laughter. Once, my name.

There were three of them. They stood, hands linked
in a spring garden. One smiled out
through her hair. Trees were ranked

behind them, dark trees, shadowing the light.
The stillness of it haunted me — if they'd moved
there would have been relief, but that

frozen dance, each foot lifting, each hand
graceful and arrogant in their drifting hair,
never changing, never coming to an end,

that was the terror, though in the bitter mirror
I saw my features shrivel out of life
and hour by hour watched all my world grow older.

They were perfect, you see, safe
with their faces no-one should possess,
no-one should have to dream of. And the knife

came to its rest among the deep green grass,
between a blue flower and a flower of gold,
opening a roaring hole of blackness,

slashing the music, slashing the silence wide;
and all the bitter certainties of art
and all my empty hours slid down inside.

Now I'll bring the chair up here; all night
I'll watch them loose their long unwinding chain.
I dare not turn my back on them again.

In a Chained Library

Here they are, chained as if dangerous,
creatures from a bestiary left open,
foxed and gilded, a tangle of tails,
mouths, claws, spilling from the shelves.

Silent as unicorns their sweet unspoken music.
Finger them, the dry crackle of their skins.
Dragons burn in margins, sea-cats uncoil;
monsters, eating letters, being letters,

as if word and flesh and beast were one
and might burst out, huge and scaly,
slithering from the nave into the crowded streets,
scorching the night with a babel of lost songs.

Scenes from a Book of Hours

December 25th
Nativity

Out in the hedges sheep turn from the wind.
Lanes are empty over the bitter hills.
Nobody travels for nobody knows the way;
today everyone will be counted where they are.
The people have hidden themselves; they've gone to ground
deep in the warm rooms and the charity halls,
burrowing into the red heart of the day,
the comfort of stories, the bright, unanswerable star.
But the heart is beating, suddenly beating
subtle and soft so the sheep look up and listen;
beating in the scarlet rotting berries;
in the tangle of the wind among the trees;
in the barn where the drunken tramp is singing;
in the corner of the church where the candles slowly stiffen.

26th
Stephen Martyr

As I spoke I saw the pain pass through them;
my words bruised like flint, and I never meant
that, only to cry aloud my certainties,
for once to be fierce and strong and sure in my heart.
Handfuls of berries were crushed as their answers felled me
and I should have known, for these are the days of blood;
juices of the hedge anointed my fingers and eyelids;
I fell through leaves and toadstools, blown snow,
and far off, as I raised my head, I saw
an empty lane that led high over hills
white with winter trees, and I longed to walk there
but darkness burst behind my eyes like joy, and deep
in the soil my fingers clutched among leaves;
the night bending over me with its splashed, spread hands.

27th
John Evangelist

To write is to make marks on the past;
distort its subtleties in hardening wax.
An old man walking in a worn-out coat,
my hands are stained with the bitter hedgerow fruit.
Who knows the writing time makes on the flesh,
the runic scrawl of water on the beach;
but I, who leaned on the shoulder of the Word,
spilled from my pen bright horsemen to trample the world?
Bard of a fisher king, I work the net,
spread imagery for your feet, try to relate
the truth of heaven to a man I once thought I loved
laughing beside me. While like a muse the wind
scribbles in powdery snow its unanswerable words;
beats at my bowed head like the heart of a bird.

28th
Childermass

How all the faces turn away from death
except the soldier's, with his lifted sword,
and the woman in the crumpled velvet dress
who lifts one hand to touch his twisted shoulder.
Here, in the fields, the grass too stiff to bend
hisses like a mass of whistling arrows;
smoke from a bonfire crackles in the hedge.
Bright berries hang, each with its secret seed
waiting to be plucked, split, pecked wide;
and some may not be born, and some may fall,
trampled into mud by the flickering boys
riding up the lanes on brand-new bikes,
flashing by field-gates like kings of a vigorous country,
fleeing to exile from the wrath of days.

29th
Thomas Becket

And all these days hang on my chamber walls
woven in frayed thread; tapestries of the tangle-
wood; the winter fields, the poor man in the lane,
the lady in her fur-lined hood. My fire of rosemary
and apple breathes its sweetness through our hearts.
Scarlet cloth, berry and thorn, and if I turned
the hanging, in the darkness and the spider webs
there'd be the weft and weave, the knotted colours,
twisted dreams, the chaos behind the eyes.
Within the hidden weaving lie our seasons,
within the web of words our mystery.
And if I were figured in a weave or poem
plashed and knotted by some glibber tongue
I could be no more tangled than I am.

The Unexplored Ocean

From the Journals of James Hartshill,
being an officer serving on His Majesty's ships
Endeavour and *Resolution*.
1768-1779

I
13th April 1769. Matavai, Oteheite.

Charlotte, I wish you could see these people!
Their ocean is blue, so blue, deeper than
the gown you wore at Rookham;
the splash and lift of it nudges the ship;
their hills an uprush of trees
mirrored in the calm lagoon where we lilt at anchor.

They came out in canoes, waving and shouting;
some of them swam, and Gore, who knows them,
swung in the rigging, laughing; the men silent
for once, lining the rails in amazement.
My sweet, the women are slim and brown,
the warriors feathered with the wings of scarlet birds.

They're all over the ship; as I write they watch,
laughing at my coat and the buckles on my shoes,
stealing, seducing, sudden and dangerous as children.
I find myself asking if this is Eden,
where sin is only the breaking of strange taboos.
The thought disturbs me, here without you.

I asked Forster if Hell was knowledge or none.
He laughed, said he had not voyaged so far,
nor hoped to. And they have given the captain
a feather cloak, and he bows so gravely.
Tomorrow he says, we unship the equipment
and six marines to guard it night and day.

It's dark now: the paper glimmers like pearl.
Already, love, the island has hold of me.
Its warm scents drift, sweet and strange,
into all the timbers of the ship; a creeping disorder,
a swaying dance. It upsets me, keeps me awake.
And I cannot laugh at myself as I would like.

II
November 1769

We deck this ocean like a princess;
hang names from her ears and throat,
bright trinkets of foreign sound.

Each point and headland receives one
— Bank's Island, Young Nick's Head —
our surnames, jokes, predicaments,

anything that happened there. Mine is the bay
I was first to see; the long blond
sweep of sand, iridescent hills

greener than green, forests
of yams and snakes and rainbow birds.
Hartshill Bay. He wrote it on the chart

in his tiny, meticulous hand.
We landed there for water. I was first.
The sand was soft, so soft and hot,

and it drifted through my fingers
like time in an hourglass.
The natives kept their distance;

we left them beads, and a few nails,
and I cut my name in a piece of wood
at the end of my footprints.

From the deck I saw the dark men
come from the trees and examine it,
turning it over and over.

III
August 1770

A man like Cook is an ocean;
you will never sail to the end of him.

You know his easy calms,
are tossed in his storms; see his determination

fling him on the world's rocks.
You'll not see under the surface,

not the currents of the heart, how they
twist and slither over wreck and pearl,

the deep gashes, fathoms drowned.
Men like this cannot uncover,

can't let the tides retreat;
do not know how to reveal, even to us that love them

what moon it is that tugs and drags them
to their ambitions' end.

IV
January 17th 1773. 67° 15' South.

We've come to the end. It's fearsome;
a wall high as the mainmast. A hard horizon.

The air is a knife in the lungs.
Speech is frozen; thought, numb.

This is as far as men can go, stumbling,
hungry, all veins breaking,

riding into fog and silence
a brittle lattice,

ropes that razor the skin,
a ship of bone.

We are frost, losing faith and fingers,
gone too far even for desires.

He faces the end of the world
and we don't ask. There are not the words.

No-one else has knocked on this closed gate;
fallen through this cleft in the heart.

His gloves tear ice from the frozen stern.
We scatter as he turns.

V
May 1773

...Recrimination has set in at last,
each saying they were only thinking of the others;
that when he turned us south and south again
their spirits had not been sick with dread.
As for me, only in these warmer seas has thought
flooded back, like blood into white veins;
only now comes feeling, the faces the cold froze out of me.
Where we were then I hardly know,
but that it was beyond where men should be.
And the long voyage back through the throb of flesh,
the release of pain, so all the body ached,
and the ship seeming to melt and soften,
dripping ice from spars and tops
into the soaking decks; the pumps churning;
the people wet to the skin and too destroyed to care.
In that extremity I felt my mind retreat,
shrivel, roll up tight, a hibernating creature;
I became cold, like the sky, like the sea,
unmoved even by my own pain, feeling death
drift by me like the white bergs in the sun.
We were close to that for sure, voyaging
into it. And now each in the gunroom says
he'd have been willing to go further, try again,
now that the winds are against us, and the foremast jacks,
eager for their women in Tahiti,
would mutiny if we tried to turn them back...

VI
June 1774. New Caledonia

Tonight, from the dark, I watch them making maps;
charting with a thin brown line the coast
we follow; laying on islands and bays and capes
the pale blue net of latitude.
The cabin is quiet; the lamp swings our shadows
left and right, easy, with the
creak of the canvas. We shift our weight
from foot to foot, balanced on the sea's back.

Pens roll on the board, scrolls of paper, thin, filmy;
inks in deep, gleaming bottles.
Strange that the line he carefully plots
is surf on sand somewhere, the fringe of a forest.
My footsteps have smudged it; a canoe breaks it with a splash.
He clears aside the sextant, dried seeds
in neat boxes; unrolls a little more
the unexplored ocean of white paper.

The world is not the same since we began.
Lands have risen from the sea, half-glimpsed
islands in the mist have hardened, become places.
Now we can see exactly where we are.
And we are the first to see them form, the strange
outlines of new continents, their white
unguessable interiors; first to see the floating islands
anchored; the dreamlands drawn out as they are.

Eight bells ring; the ship wears with the wind.
Clerke coughs into his handkerchief,
wipes one dark spot carefully from the chart.
He'll never get back to England and he knows it,
he's plotting his own voyage into nowhere
and all of us with him, as far as we can go,
into the whiteness, the silence and the cold.
But tonight, we are the first to see the world.

VII
July 1774

Under studding-sails we make eight knots,
slicing the white water.
Sitting here in the swinging top
I see sharks, two grey slithers

in the immense blue circle of the sea.
The wind tears my hair
and shirt; one arm holds me
rolling in the wild, wild air.

A day when it's good just to be racing;
nothing happening but speed,
the sails straining and billowing
as if I'm a bird, above clouds,

and from here I can see them all
as they make and mend, knotting and splicing,
shirts hanging to dry on the rails,
neckerchiefs flapping.

There's Gibson, darning his collar,
Clerke, Edmondson,
Forster, smoking, arguing about fauna
with his diffident son.

They should be remembered; there should
be some praise for them;
suffering the great man's hardships
without his acclaim,

and the people, too, with their fierce pride
at going further, at naming
bays after their sweethearts; who'll find
their mark but the mapmakers to come?

Only they know the ocean is so mighty
that tomorrow nothing will be changed.
We'll still be a white ship on the empty sea
as if we'd raced all day and never moved.

VIII

Anger burns me, phosphorescent
in my fist. All day I've held it tight
in case it lessens. "Captain's compliments"
he said, and the others watched me go, into the square
of cabin, the swinging light, his curt
recital of my faults. Gore was there,
with one of his covert looks. Now
I hang over the rail and the water is black
as my thoughts, and there's nowhere to go
or be alone in this ramshackle chariot
creaking round the globe. Here in the dark
I wonder where we're going, into what
deep seas of ourselves living like this will drive us;
who'll be the first to smash the glass of the compass.

IX
1778

I took some men and found James Harrison
lying between two women in a hut,
his hair stuck full of flowers, dressed like an indian.

There have been desertions. The Captain
in his savage mood, burned canoes;
the constant thieving drives him to distraction.

He's crippled by his back. To our deep delight
twelve great Tahitian women massaged him.
At least now he sleeps easier at night.

He offered to leave Clerke there on the island,
said he should not sail into the ice,
but knew he'd come. None of us would

leave him now, despite his rages.
Yesterday I thought of Charlotte, for no reason,
sitting in the garden with the boys,

telling them of me, wondering where I am.
Their faces were blurs. Desire to see them
made me grip the stays, an almost bodily pain.

We sail north. The sails and mast are rotten.
He swears he'll have the hides of those in Deptford.
Everyone knows that somehow our luck has gone.

The Tahitians spoke of an island in the ocean,
a place of strange beliefs.
It would be good to eat fresh meat again...

Pen raised, I hear the surging of the sea;
Discovery to windward, like a shadow,
someone playing a fiddle, quietly...

X
February 1779. Hawaii

...Today at last they gave us his remains; we saw
them carried in a wild procession;
his bones, God help us, and a few rags of his coat;
no-one will tell that to Elizabeth.
I feel sick; sick and lost and wretched, but that's it,
that's how men are. King told us
that they thought he was some god,
that they keep asking when he will come back.
Sometimes I turn at a footstep and almost believe it.
I can't remember what is right, what the rain
feels like at Greenwich in November;
I can't remember all the places that I've been.
Somewhere I travelled into someone different,
grew new thoughts and scars, even a new past —
I'm afraid no-one will know me now at home;
even Charlotte will give one glance over my shoulder,
searching for the boy she thought she knew.
We have explored, and everything has changed;
we have gone too far and seen too much,
have been forever sailing, sailing to this,
and where do you go after death, after striking
that rock?
    Now in the cabin they argue;
Clerke's ill, coughing his life out, but we'll go on
he says, we'll go north, it's what the captain
would have wanted. He's right, it doesn't matter;
we need the cold, the numbness, the adversity;
we need it before England and the rain,
the women waiting on the dock,
the unanswerable questions about Cook,
who found there was no end to any journey;
that there is always somewhere else to go....

Acknowledgements

Some of these poems have appeared in the following publications:
Acumen, Poetry Wales, Poetry Review, Planet, The New Welsh Review,
the *Western Mail, The Bright Field* (Carcanet).